silent no more

a collection of poetry

Edited by
John M. Grohol

Table of Contents

Introduction

A collection of poetry is a rare and special thing, often held together by some common thread. This book is one that embodies the essence of emotions — of feelings pure and true, poured out within these pages by a group of people who's only connection is an online support community.

The idea for this book was obvious in retrospect. For four years, I've been honored to host this online support community and within it, a place for members to share their creative side. Over the years, the forum has seen hundreds upon hundreds of works of poetry posted to it. This first collection is a volunteer effort that wouldn't have been possible without the contributions of dozens of authors that appear within these pages.

Proceeds from this book will be used to help establish a fund that will disburse small "life grants." It is hoped these grants will help members of our online support community better their lives in some small but meaningful fashion.

The title of this collection was inspired by the long silence many people suffering from mental health issues have had to endure throughout their lives. Speaking up about abuse, depression, anxiety, suicide, trauma — these are never easy things to talk about. It is far easier to remain quiet, to not make waves. By breaking the silence, these authors give hope to anyone who's ever suffered from mental illness.

I am proud and honored to put together this special collection of poetry for your consideration. All of these poems are worthy, and many will touch your heart. If you enjoy this collection, please let us know by writing to:

poetry@psychcentral.com

The online support community that brought these creative souls together is Psych Central, available at:

http://forums.psychcentral.com/

John M. Grohol
Founder, Psych Central

A new life

Our life began a long time ago.
We both have loved.
We both have lived hard lives.
But can we overcome this to begin a new life with each other?
I think we can.
I love you,
You love me.
You are my other half,
You are my soul mate.
I want you in my life forever.
Our love should be bonded like no other
We should commit ourselves while we can.
We should love like no other has loved us.
Our love grows stronger ever day.
We create a new life each day we love.
I love you with all my heart and soul.
Marry me, marry me forever.

- *Patricia Bell*

Like a Child

Like a child
She has a heart that's good
Like all people should
Like a child,
She only wants to have fun.
And loves nearly everyone.
Like a child, she tries to do what's right,
And always is polite.
Like a child,
She would do anything to make you smile.
For that's her style.
She's the pride and joy,
Of every little boy.

- *Angie Harmon*

Trust Broken

I hurt myself so you can't,
Don't you understand?
I can't just stop cutting,
Because you demand.
That little girl is still trapped,
In this body of mine.
I don't care what you say,
It's not going to be fine.
I had to take the abuse,
I was the one raped.
God look at me,
I still haven't escaped!
I trusted them all,
But what do they do?
Take my innocence,
Still waiting to be rescued.
Can't you see now,
It has nothing to do with you?
I'm sorry I can't trust you,
I just have to hurt me before you do.

- *Stacy Roach*

There's Hope

We share our stories sad and true
sometimes we don't know what to do
we cry we moan we wail and whine
we even lose all track of time
our friends stick by us while we heal
they understand our pain is real
they know we must express that pain
in order to feel whole again
depression such lonely place
where all of us have shown our face
we hold our head up as we try
to grab some hope as it goes by
and if at first we don't succeed
we'll try again and then indeed
we shall get well we will be glad
we need not be forever sad
I wish that we could vow tonight
to share our strengths and hold on tight
to take each other by the hand
to help each other understand
there's hope for all.

-    *Susan King*

Broken Heart

Three long years you prayed for me
How you felt I couldn't see
You thought your prayers were said alone
You'll never know that I had known
In the pit of my despair
You alone were always there
When I felt like I should die
You held me close and dried my eyes
When life was over from the guilt
You showed me how I could rebuild
I wasn't there when your father died
I tried to hold you when you cried
But I was lost within myself
Was not aware I needed help
You were always there for me
But for you I couldn't be
Three long years you rode my ride
While every day more of you died
You took the worst without a frown
And never let it get you down
But now it's time for you to go
And I pray to God this isn't so
You'll never know how much I care
You only know I wasn't there
In our lives you're not guilt free
But it's mostly 'cause of me
I've made my bed so here I lie
While everything inside had died
I know we can't go back again
I'm lucky if you'll be my friend
Now I'm left here all alone
In this place that's not my home
Time to fix this broken heart
But I don't know where to start

-    *Ryan McMahon*

Knowledge is Truth

Fear is the enemy that imprisons our soul,
Guilt is the enemy that makes us grow cold.
Now is the time to realize,
the meaning of paradise.
Where love is shining in our eyes,
now we can be healed.
Love lies in understanding our friends and our foes,
Love is the way of healing the fear and guilt we know.
Knowledge is the truth that gives light to our darkness.

-    *Angie Harmon*

I Knew

Maybe it's up
Maybe it's down

Maybe I'm right
Maybe you are wrong

Maybe I can speak
Maybe I can show

Take a breath
Take a moment
Take a chance
Take a challenge

Show me I'm right
Show me I'm not wrong to feel

He said I knew what I did
There is no reason to speak
I knew what I had done

- *Lisa L. Turner*

The Sale

Sweating in the hot, hot sun.
Cannot stop 'till work is done.
No water, no food, take the rays
If I live to see another day.

Three tons of sand sit on the dirt
Move it carefully or I get hurt.
Drop the shovel, drop some sand,
I'll be hit by hard, cruel hand.

He sits on chaise in the shade
Making sure no mistakes are made.
Eating food, drinking iced Diet Rite,
Laughing and yelling to do it right.

A truck pulls up not far from me.
A man watches with lust filled glee.
Evil dark eyes glitter under hat brim.
He's sick and sadistic, I'm sure of him.

He shouts to father that he wants one,
The kind who can get hard work done.
Father laughs loud with crazy glee.
Says he might consider selling me.

Sand forgotten, I lean on the shovel
Listening to the two Satin's devils
Who bicker and barter in front of me.
I know I just work, that I'm not free.

I realize if I am bought,
I must fight and not get caught.
Shovel is all I have with me
To defend myself and then to flee.

I feel the hard shovel in my hands.
I shift my feet to make a stand.
There's no safe haven anywhere.
Many know, but they don't care.

I'll run fast and I'll run far,
But can't outrun father's car.
I wonder if I'll hear the crack
When he shoots me in the back.

If I'm lucky he'll shoot me in the head.
At least I should be quickly dead.
Hear man refuse to pay father's demand.
Realize I will stay in this Hell's land.

Sweating in the hot, hot sun.
Cannot stop 'till work is done.
No water, no food, take the rays
If I am to live another day.

-     *Bonnie O'Hara*

Reluctant Compliance

Like punching a patronizing time clock
I execute an act of pharmacological faith
So that this fractured brain
Can function undetected by the insensitive.

I engage in a daily skirmish
Battling urges of defiance, pride, and denial
Only conquering non-compliance with sobering
Memories of manic ruin and Bedlam's misery.

So, with a perfunctory glance,
A medicinally modified mind
Turns, parting from the mirror's defeated reflection,
Fortified, to face the day.

- *Christopher Hall*

Crocs

Reptile-headed hipsters
Clenched unfiltered Camels
In smug and cruel
Crocodile smiles.
Smoke crawled along scaly snouts
Under the pitiless white glare
Of sodium-arc street lamps
Arrayed along a curb
Littered with discarded
Hypodermics and condoms.

I exhaled smoke
Into the damp night air,
Slouched against a wall of bricks
Stacked and mortared
Like the discolored, discarded teeth of
giants,
Before crushing the spent cartridge
Of nicotine
Under a steel-toed motorcycle boot.
Acid-Addled Walter still kneeled
unsteadily
Amid the puddles
On the alley's asphalt stage,
The vomit on his shirt
And jeans already dried and caked.
I lit another Marlboro to mask the stink
Of decay that seemed to emerge
With every labored breath he took.

Random beads of jewel-like water
Clung to my black leather Buffalo jacket,
Tiny rainbow-hued prisms
That seemed out of place
Amid the scuffed sleeves
And unraveling seams.
A faint spray of ash
Tumbled from the glowing ember
At the end of my cigarette,
Dusting my ratty Dead Kennedys t-shirt
With a fine coat of tainted snow.
Tendrils of smoke explored
The spaces among the eruption
Of spiked brown hair atop my head.
The music from the club
Throbbed lazily in my ears
As it made its escape
Through the fire exit.

In the distance
A shriveled figure approached,
Appearing and vanishing,
Vanishing and appearing,
As she moved along the sidewalk
From one pool of light to the next.

Her five-foot frame
Inched slowly past
The glowing predator eyes
Of the herd down the street
With the palsied, leaden tread
Of doomed prey.
The flickering orange of their cigs
Moved to follow her progress
Like a swarm
Of choreographed fireflies.

She glanced up into my face,
Her skin gray and stretched
Too tightly over her
Tiny skull,
Her arms bruised, purple,
Punctuated with the Morse code
markings
Of too many needles.
I met her gaze
With the practiced jaded indifference
So prized by teenagers.
No more than 15, I mused,
She's no more than 15.

A clatter from the alley
As Acid-Addled Walter
Tottered to his feet,
Toppling the lid of a garbage can
Onto the ground
During his uncertain ascent
Back into consciousness.
She jumped, startled, hollow eyes wide,
Pleading.
I held out my box of Marlboro reds,
Striking a match as she drew
The cigarette to her lips
With quivering hands, old woman's
hands.
She took a drag,
Then continued her tenuous pilgrimage
Past me and into the night.
What did we each see? I wondered.
Her past? My future?
I nodded to Acid-Addled Walter
That it was time to go
And we slid away
From the other crocs
On the concrete riverbank,
Saying nothing, thinking everything.

-    *The Cheshire Cat*

The Pain is There

I hate to think back, remember the past
The dark clouds there are always cast
The pain is there

There are so many memories of broken hearts
Some sad and hurting, some cold and hard
The pain is there

Hurting children crying, unsure of themselves
Lying in the dark you can hear their wails
The pain is there

Such uncertainty and fear of what will come
Spirits are battered and broken, innocence is gone
The pain is there

Terror I see when I look into their eyes
So bewildered and confused, always asking why
The pain is there

I try to help them, but I can't you see
Because one of the crying children is me
And pain is there…

Can I ever help the children?

- *Kim Helton*

Living in the Past

Living in the past won't do;
We have to go on,
We have to go through.

No one lives in the gathered stories,
Telling what we can and cannot do;
What will and will not fail.
The standing past is dead to us, though
It is all we think we know.

Living in the past won't do;
We have to go on,
We have to go through.

The past is another country.
As Lowell says: it is a stage play
Issuing no tickets, playing eternally
Elsewhere.

Living in the past won't do;
We have to go on,
We have to go through.
The standing past is dead to us, though
It is all we think we know.

The standing past is dead;
A dead thing to let go.
We have to go on,
We have to go through,
And so we do -
But still we take the past
That lives in us and not
The thing we think we know.

-    *Myzen*

Will You Want Me Here

When I can't remember you may I stay a while
when my memory fades will I be welcome
when I've forgotten those whom I hold dear
will you want me here

When this demon creeps and crawls into my mind
when I forget to be who I am now
when I forget all those who have been kind
will you want me here

When I've changed and you can't recognize me
and I no longer even speak your name
when you need distance 'tween yourself and me
will you want me here

When the Alzheimers' leaves me weak and helpless
and I lie here all curled up upon the bed
when you remember dear that once you loved me
will you want me here

-    *Susan King*

That Curious Larder Door

She tugged repeatedly
at that refrigerator door
It would slam mightily
each time her name was called.

Intently, she'd return
to entrance that held her captive
would turn and grin blue flashes
as she opened such forbidden portal.

When her name was mentioned
she'd quickly put it back
Disarm me with her giggle
run and hug my leg.

Dinner being consumed
All her green sides done
I hesitantly relented, freed
that verboten door.

She happily took me
to the stuff of her endearment
Without hesitation, picked
the biggest of the bunch.

I sliced and peeled
the fruit of her desire
till there was nothing left
of that forbidden pulpy mass

Next day when I hungered
I opened that curious larder door
As I reached for daily sustenance
I neatly found each apple
With just one nibble gone

-       *Tomi Inglis*

Cobain au Café du Monde, 1994

Brain full of napalm
Lights incandescent flames
That flash like gas jets
Behind my blue eyes.

Loping along Bourbon Street,
Sipping a pina colada
In a Slurpee cup.
Bopping in syncopated time
To the zydeco
Blasting from open barroom doors
As the rapid-fire Cajun-flavored patois
Of ruddy-faced hustlers,
Preaching on the sidewalks,
Seeks to save the souls
Of any sober pilgrims
By luring them inside
To the bar-stool pews.
But the warm shrimp Po' Boy
Sitting in my stomach
Has me feeling too mellow
To listen.

Neon in the windows,
Tubes of glowing gas,
Cast multi-hued reflections
On the tattoo,
Freshly polished to a sheen
With cocoa butter,
Of an Irish Celtic knot
That adorns my inner right wrist.

Elissa on my left,
My wife of 18 months,
A lyrical moving swirl
Of psychedelic tie-dye
And ankle-length orange peasant skirt.
Shoulder-length blond hair
Flows behind her

As she takes a hit
Of a strawberry daiquiri
In an innocuous
Wax-paper cup
Topped with a plastic lid and straw.
Wearing as many
Gaudy plastic beaded necklaces
As 10 bucks will buy,
Which is a lot.

Tokin' Tiny Tim
Trotting to my right
Like an agitated terrier
Trying to keep pace
With my lanky stride.
His buzz cut
Bobbing up,
Bobbing down,
Like a marker buoy
In a current of humid flesh that
Exhales booze-scented sweat
Through every pore.

I'm draped
In basic warm-weather Goth,
Black t-shirt,
Black jeans,
Black cowboy boots
Ringed at the ankles
With silver chains
That jingle like
A gunslinger's spurs
With every step.
My hair, as usual, a halo of spikes,
A dark yang
To Elissa's bright yin.

I've got just enough hippie
And she's got just enough punk
To make the thing work.

Acid-Addled Walter is MIA,
Took off with a vampire chick
To get fitted for custom-made fangs
Made by a local dentist
As a sideline.
Anne Rice and Lestat
Are the two biggest names
In town.
Walter and batgirl
Hooked up
In a second-story
Punk/goth shop,
Where I bought a new
Black t-shirt
With the classic anarchy symbol
From the late '70s.

It nestles in my backpack
Next to the first-edition Faulkner,
"New Orleans Sketches,"
That I slapped down a Franklin for
In the tiny bookstore
Tucked away in Pirate's Alley
That had been the author's apartment
When he hammered out his first novel.

Tokin' Tiny Tim
Thought I was nuts
To spend that much
On a book.
I'd try to explain,
But he'll never understand.
Never seen a pothead
Who was such a bundle
Of nerves,
Drifting through life
In a cloud of cannabis smoke,
Babbling neurotically
Like Woody Allen.
Says I make him edgy,
Never knows what I'll say,
Never knows what I might do,
Accuses me of having
No impulse control,
And hell, I can't
Really argue with that.

Cops on horseback
Move serenely among the crowd.
Every night they seal off
Bourbon
From traffic
With huge antique iron
stanchions
Covered with peeling paint,
And the nightcrawlers emerge,
Whores and poets,
Tourists and addicts,
To traipse and strut and dance
Across the macadam ballroom.

The decapitated noggins
Of a million baby alligators,
Lacquered and preserved
With jaws agape,
Stare forlornly
From every souvenir shop
display
That I see,
And this is too debauched
Even for me,
To sell the heads of infants
As trinkets
While bellowing,
"Laissez les bon temps rouler."

Sun's coming up.
I imagine Acid-Addled Walter
Curled up in the arms
Of his vampire lover
Someplace dark
And lined
With crimson silk.
"Let's hit the Café du Monde,"
I say,
So we head west
Toward the Mississippi,
And eventually I feel
The first rays of the dawn
Prickling the skin
On the back of my neck.

I stop at a drop-box
To buy a copy
Of the Times-Picayune
And take a sucker-punch
To the gut
When I read the headline
At the bottom of the page:
"Singer Kurt Cobain Found Dead"

He'd slipped away from a rehab clinic
To a room above his garage,
Scribbled
"I'm sorry
I'm sorry
I'm sorry"
On a piece of paper,
Shot up some smack,
Followed by a chaser
Of shotgun shells
To his brain.

Why is this hitting me so hard?
I wonder.
Yes, Nirvana is
My favorite band.
Yes, "Nevermind" is
My favorite album.
But just as a moment
Of insight
Seems within reach,
It slips away
As Tokin' Tiny Tim
Blurts,
"It had to happen
Sooner or later."

I turn to face him
With a feral rage
That I don't really understand,
Snarling,
"Shut up, goddamn it,
Just shut the hell up."

Sitting sullenly at a table
Under the green and white striped
awning,
Facing away from the café's
Cheery sunburst yellow stucco facade.
I snatch up my plate of beignets,
Sending a plume of the white powdered
sugar
Atop them
Wafting across the small round table,
And stalk across the street,
Clutching a cup of French Roast coffee
In my other hand.
"Why is he always so moody?"
I hear Tokin' Tiny Tim
Ask Elissa.

I climb the steps
Along the concrete floodwall
To the ancient Spanish cannon
At the top
And slump against the muzzle pointing
out
At the chocolate milk waters
Of the Mississippi delta.
I bite into a sweet, sweet beignet,
Wash it down with coffee,
And begin
Humming "Heart-Shaped Box"
To the gulls.

-    *The Cheshire Cat*

Black Hole

Nothing held
Nothing wanted

Nothing Loved
Nothing cared for

Nothing given
Nothing taken

Nothing asked for
Nothing excepted

Nothing needed
Nothing offered

Nothing seen
Nothing spoken

Nothing known
Everything Lost

- *Lisa L. Turner*

Shell

Many entities
Trapped in a shell
Nowhere to go
Nowhere to hide

Restless they are
Paralyzed with fear
Smothered voices
Silent screams

Then all is still
Nothing left
Gone
Just an empty shell

-    *SS8282*

Come Back To Me

I think about you all the time,
Do you ever think about me?
I remember all the little things,
Like how you made me feel free.
No matter how big or small I was,
You told me I was beautiful.
You made me feel as if,
I were your beautiful angel.
I know I took your love for granted,
I know it's my fault we're not together now.
I wish I could bring us back together,
Is there a way? Tell me how.
I miss you so much,
I wish you missed me too.
I wish you could take away my sadness,
Like you always used to do.
Tell me you still love me,
Tell me there's still a chance.
I'll do whatever it takes,
To bring back this romance.
Is she better than me,
Does she know the real Bo?
Please tell me she doesn't,
That its only me who knows.
I love you and I miss you,
I'm still waiting for you yet.
I'll be here waiting forever,
Because you I can not forget.

-    *Stacy Roach*

My Am

Out of step and out of sync
Is how I've always been
And I am not the one you think
You've known since way back when

That one's a uniform I've worn
To blend into the scene
The me the way that I was born
Is there behind a screen

Afraid to step out front to show
The rhythm of my Am
Which does not match the general flow
And tends to get me slammed

My uniform is threadbare, though
And peppered now with holes
And I'm not sure that I can sew
Another for my soul

So, naked now, and out of step
I try to make my way
Back to the Am that I have kept
So neatly stashed away

But Am and I have been apart
For such a length of time
I'm not quite sure just where to start
To reclaim Am as mine.

-    *Julie Gordon*

Love Defined

Love is not found in a dictionary,
defining the certain criteria.
It is not found in an age, a number to signify years one has passed the
sun in the earths rotation.
Love can not be defined by a judge, a counselor, a warden, a mother, or
anyone else.
Love can not be defined by teachers or scholars or philosophers.
Love can only be felt and known.
There is no limitation whether it is a number or a distance.
It is either there or it is not.
It can not be taken away by anyone other than the one who feels it.

-    *Vulgerlove*

Big Sky Blue

I'm headin' west across Montana,
I'm steerin' with my knees,
Groovin' on Santana,
Twistin' up some leaves.

I got a heart as big as Texas,
And love enough to paint the sky;
It's like a moon that only waxes,
I guess I'll never know quite why.

Life's so full of sweet distraction,
And can leave you sad and spent...
If we let go of satisfaction,
Could we hold our heart's content?

I want to be just like the dancer,
learn to flow instead of strive...
It's the question not the answer
That keeps our hearts alive.

I'm headin' east across Montana,
Feelin' big sky blue,
I only hope this old Impala
Can get me home to you.

- *Sqrlb8*

Imposter

I first met Jaromir at the University. He looked
Like a philosophy professor, but was just a harmless
Imposter keeping warm in the lecture theatres.
A Polish subject under Hitler once, he had a
Careful presence, and spoke his perfect English
Quietly. I smiled at him there
And then and we were friends.

Sometimes, in the formal lectures, he would
Be drawn fatally to ask a question of a
Real professor. Student's eyes would turn towards
Him, massive in his person. He sat stiffly upright, with the
Sunlight glinting on the row of shiny pens lined in his suit
Pocket- like soldiers. He couldn't hide his difference in his
Eloquence. We all knew that he should not be here and his
Questions, exactly pertinent, only made that more
Clear. He was too intelligent for the undergraduates.

Of course I brought him
Home; his loneliness catching on
Mine, his survival my model.
He trimmed his nails in our kitchen
Marking his temporary ground.
He took me to the place where he slept, in
Leigh Woods in a small hollow. I could barely
See the outline where his body had lain in
The dry grass, like a shadow. He told me
That he slept there quite well. He had been nervous
At first but comfortable, and he had radio 3 on headphones
To pass the evenings under his plastic sheeting. He said that
He tried carefully to blend in, that he wouldn't be seen if
Someone walked too near, but that there was a
Problem with dogs, which I hadn't thought of
But now seems obvious.

When he went his homeless way he left some things
With us, wobbled on his rusty bike to the
End of the street, round the last corner and
Was gone forever. I looked through his stuff again
The other day. There was a picture of the family
He said he hated, two women very old even then
And his small face there, ghostlike.
There was a box of paper squares;
Single characters drawn in Japanese with such care,
Using brush and pen; there were hundreds of them.
Each white sheet had been marked with
Quick lines just once.

The marks were delicate, so
Like him that I was shaken;
They were as clear and definite
As the mark he'd left on me.

-    *Myzen*

Another Dream

waking windows, watching clear blue skies
over the mountains and high above the trees
sun shines through, asking for an entry
into your heart—the beating stops.

into your mind, you fall forward with a heave
looking for something to grasp hold of
yet finding nothing of substance
you tumble downward, through the darkness.

landing on a cool springy bed of moss
you look around to discover a breeze
flowing through your hair
and asks who you are.

you do not know.

> the breeze stops.

> > the moss whithers.

> > > and still, you fall.

-   *John M. Grohol*

Heaven's Gate

Well there's always
somebody sayin',
sayin' they're sure I'm
quite insane and
sayin' I'm playin',
playin' with fire,
ooh, with fire
and with pain.
Oh,
but I say thunder,
thunder and lightning...
don't they seem like
one and the same?
And now they're duckin'
outta sight from,
from blue skies
a pourin' rain.

I ain't sayin' that I know more than you do,
but I know just what I know
and I know
that it's true.

All I'm really sayin' is, I love you,
really love you.

Aw, you're livin'
all alone and
you're just waiting
in the wings.
And in your own mind,
you're performing
such fantastic amazing scenes.
But when you finally,
finally awaken,
well don't it seem like
the oddest thing,
to find your odyssey,
odyssey ending
as the fat lady sings?

I ain't sayin' that I know more than you do,
but I know just what I know
and I know
that it's true.

All I'm really sayin' is, I love you,
really love you.

You know it ain't like,
like it's too late now;
hell is only
what we create.
You don't even
have to wait,
no,
nobody's burden
is too great.
Liberate and
free your own mind,
by simply droppin'
all your hate.
We can leave it,
leave it behind us,
and together
storm heaven's gate.

I ain't sayin' that I know more than you do,
but I know just what I know,
and I know
that it's true.

All I'm really sayin' is, I love you,
really love you.
All I'm ever sayin' is, I love you...

-     *Sqrlb8*

- 39 -

Cedar

'Tis a comfort
wake up near to buried in cedar boughs, face full of mud
to sight of Tom's leg then spark of his pipe lit.

He beside me, guide, wide, with those forest eyes.
"No day in the park, to have your bones picked clean."
Some sort of cough and sputter from me in response, affirm.

Where was I where am I? I'm up, world sways then rights.
Twigs out of hair, there's silvered scales on my jeans, right, I was
salmon.

Hand to cedar trunk, thunk of connect.
I stand and slide into cedar.
Tom grins and puffs.
I'm treed.

All good in the wood.
Hire a guide, best is one inside.
And listen to me: Hansel and Gretel lied.

-    *Sarah Light*

Mortality

Where you born on your first breath?
Or did God give you this life for-ever-more?
How do you perceive your death?

He gives our parents the gift of life.
He can end peace, or start a war?
But can he break down people in strife?

Is your life full of light or darkness?
Has your soul been shattered and scorned?
Do you live a life of barren starkness?

Do you find a blessed peace?
Or has your whole life been forlorn?
Watching for those who fleece?

- *Patricia Bell*

The Cloud

The cloud approaches, cold, dark, and familiar.
My walk in the sunshine has been nice, yet I don't belong there.
Dark is real. The cloud is real, and it calls to me.
I would like to surrender to its familiar embrace, to once more
experience the depth of feeling that only the cloud brings.
Sunshine is warm, but it will never last. Night comes always.

Still, I remember what it was like, life inside the cloud.
Cold and misery set in and soon grow oppressive.
Soon I would forget how sunshine feels.
There would be naught but the cloud,
    and I would not remember to search for light.
Though at first seeking feeling and depth, I would grow numb and
    uncaring, withdrawn from the world outside,
        stuck inside the cloud.

Who will search for me in the cloud and help me escape?
    Will anyone notice my absence?
The only way for me to break free of my prison is to feel again.
    The only thing I can feel is pain.

Why does the cloud call to me, appear attractive to me?
    Why do I long to go to it? Do I have a choice?
    How does one live in the sunshine?

-    *Rapunzel*

Street Cinderella

Street Cinderella's pluckin'
Shards of glass from her feet,
Razor bits of busted slippers
Back from when she was sweet,
A fairy tale turned pale
And I watch her petite
Waif's face braced in pain,
Worn and scuffed with defeat,
Ashen eyes monochrome
As she daydreams of elite
Suitors sittin' on her bench
And askin' her to meet
For a drink on the brink
Of a romance so fleet
That she blushes, breathless,
At the way they all treat
Her like the queen of the prom
Who makes hearts skip a beat.
Yellowed gown, dime-store crown,
Just wants to be discreet,
Doesn't feel the cold,
Doesn't feel the heat,
Scans her Washington Square kingdom
Built of bones and concrete.
The last page is torn out,
And her story incomplete,
No prince, no goddamn castle,
Just a splintered wooden seat
Past the edge of everything
Where the ghost-walkers retreat.

-    *The Cheshire Cat*

Disintegration

I am dissolving into a thing that I don't understand
What surrounds me confounds me; and I don't know what I am
Except that what I was before is not what I will be
When this Disintegration Beast has had its way with me.

I have been the Watcher part of one who cannot stay
Within herself, and when she's gone the Watcher saves the day
By remote control I move the body and dictate the speech
Of the Shell she's left behind her when she's drifted out of reach

But now I smell the wretched stench of the Beast who will lay waste
To Watcher, Soul and Shell, all three, to satisfy its taste
For weakness (and we can't resist it in our current state)
Disintegration is its mission---now it is our fate

A Watcher is emotionless, and a Soul adrift can't care
And poor old Shell can't sense Disintegration's hungry stare
Perhaps we should go quietly---dissolve away with grace
And find out then if we'll become more than an aftertaste.

-    *Julie Gordon*

Another One

I still remember
when they laid him away;
you're so much like him
you better watch what you say.

Folks around here,
they kill what they fear;
and they're afraid of everything
you hold dear.

Turn your lights off
and keep your shades pulled down.
Word is gettin' out now
it's all over town.

They say you're the one
who knows love is true;
they got pitch forks and torches
and they're comin' for you.

Well, good luck to you son,
I sure hope you make it.
The one before you was strong
but he couldn't take it.

- *Sqrlb8*

Voices

Orange glow of roadside light
Pale haze on the street at night
Cloudy fog obscures the moon
Sends a chill of impending doom
Eerie moonlight from above
This place was never touched by love
Forgotten road runs through the wood
There's no escape, no one could
Wispy willows bend in the breeze
Shadows move about the trees
Shadows cast from things unseen
Twisted shapes, grotesque... obscene
Familiar image... horror scene
Off somewhere a muffled scream
Cold sharp breeze upon the face
Shiver inside and quicken the pace
In the ears a sound is heard
There's no one there... the thought's
                                    absurd
Whispering voices from thin air
On the nerves they start to wear
Whispering things one shouldn't hear
They do not fall upon deaf ears
Reality or just a dream
Repeated is that wretched scream

Voices speak of worthlessness
And how his life's become a mess
There's no way out, no joy, no hope
There's no way left for him to cope
End it all to be set free
"Nothing more for you to be"
End it now to kill the pain
Tears begin to flow like rain
Lying fetal 'neath the haze
Staring out with cold blank gaze
Racked inside with fear and doubt
Voices start to scream and shout
Shake's his head to calm them down
Back to a whisper is the sound
Demonic voice of pain and hate
Demons anxious at the gate
Rocking back and forth with care
No one came to save him there
Deep inside is found the will
To stand back up and face the chill
Long dark road to walk alone
He prays to God He'll soon be home

-    *Ryan McMahon*

life

when life feels like a treadmill
stop walking and look around
you will discover things you never saw before
friends family who care
you thought there was nothing there
think of the good
and of the bad
then walk a little further
stop, look around
things were not as bad as you thought
that is life my friend

-    *Simon Raistrick*

Angel wings above

She was my angel
She is my guardian angel now
she watches over me night and day

She is my grandmother
I have not seen her in many years
I can still feel her in my life
I loved her with my heart
I loved her deeply
Deeper than I love myself

For she was and is my guardian angel
My grandmother, My angel
My one and only "nana"
I love her with all my heart
I can sense her in my life
with all that I do
I can sense her in my daily routine protecting me from harm
She is my inspiration
She is my light
She is one of many who watch over me
She is one of many who care for me in the "afterlife"
She is one of many whom I seek in my advice

My angel above
Answer my call
I need to feel you again
I am missing your thoughts
I am missing your prayers'
I am missing your love and warmth

For all I feel is cold, cold darkness
In my life
Let me be, free once again To love
Let me feel your love again
Let me hear the sparrow sing her happy song
Let me hear the rabbits making sweet love under the brush
Let me hear spring all around
Let the warmth warm the scales on my wings
Let my wings soar high once again
To watch over the ones I love

Grandma, your dragon is hurting
Grandma, she is seeking your advice, Help her.. Once again

-    *Patricia Bell*

The Road to Nowhere

On the road to nowhere
Everything looks the same
As if going in circles
On a straight line

Full of dirt and gravel
Nothing but brown and grey
Choking on the blowing sand
Shriveling from the beating sun

Every gas station
Has the same name
Every truck stop
Has the same menu

Every face seems familiar
Yet no signs of recognition
Everyone speaks the same language
Only they can understand

Songs on the radio
So eerie and sad
Plays to the beat
Of the pounding heart

All alone on the road
In between stops
Staring straight ahead
Blind to the view

Sun transforms into moon
Then back again
Time has come and gone
But everything stays the same

Over the horizon
With no end in sight
Reality and illusion merges
Driving on the road to nowhere

- *SS8282*

Victorian Crusades of the 21st Century

Their pet they named Rote
And called it by habit—but wild

The pioneers placed it at the Church
Of Good Carpets and strident

They bitched "it has worn us out by the
Foot and past measure!"

Said the apothecary Dr. Phil
"We'll dose it together."

But it takes turds in its mouth
Into the parlor of our house

He charged "Let it . . .
With each nugget is clay so its

Expected one day it will shit
An Adam upon this Eve."

Restore order and domestication
By winded mastication
As clay wears the enamel
From our own teeth

At this Nurse Beatle broke from
Stroking it and to them an aside

Cut and dry she whispered
"My Dears the dump you make
is equal to the dung
you take"

    -   *Kathyanita*

A Piece of Me

When you passed me on the street,
And did not even bother to speak,
You took a piece of me.

When you saw me lonely and sad,
And did not try to comfort me,
You took a piece of me.

When you saw me struggling with life,
And did not offer an encouraging word,
You took a piece of me.

When you saw me beaten down,
And did not try to lift me up,
You took a piece of me.

When you saw I had no one to lean on,
And you chose to turn away,
You took a piece of me.

When you took all the pieces I had left,
I turned and cried out to the Father,
"Why have they forsaken me?"

The Father replied to me,
"I sent my Son to save the world,
And they took a piece of Me.

When they beat and persecuted Him,
And offered Him no relief,
They took a piece of Me.

When they nailed Him to the cross,
And gave Him vinegar for His thirst,
They took a piece of Me.

When My Son cried out from the cross,
"Father, why have you forsaken Me,?"
They took a piece of Me.

When they punctured His side,
To see that He was dead,
They took a piece of Me.

When I gave my Son for you to have life,
And through Him find comfort and love,
I gave you a piece of Me.

When I gave you all that I could,
By giving you My only Son,
I gave you a piece of Me.

When you are struggling, lonely, and sad,
Remember the sacrifice I made,
When I gave you a piece of Me."

- *Sharon Cook*

It's Too Dark, Love

Walking on sidewalks
In the twilight
Of a Hendrix
Purple haze,
My eyes crawl
On the concrete
As I avert my
Pilgrim's gaze,
From the pulsing
Anguished face
Of the sun's
Dying rays.

Bad mojo's floating free,
But I just inhale the stuff,
It's too dark, love,
But never dark enough.

Homeless in
Cardboard bunkers,
Silent regrets, their
Tongueless phrase.
The whores
Strut to slowing
Mercedes in
Competing displays.
Times Square titans
Open eyes of light
For the suckers
They'll amaze.

Bad mojo's floating free,
But I just inhale the stuff,
It's too dark, love,
But never dark enough.

And I miss
Your soft whispers,
Spider silk bejeweled
With morning dew,
Fleshly taste
Of entwined fingers,
Scent of rain all
About you.
Slap of your
Purple sandals,
Your fading steps,
Sharp and true.

Bad mojo's floating free,
But I just inhale the stuff,
It's too dark, love,
But never dark enough.

-    *The Cheshire Cat*

Abject Sadness

From off in the distance,
it watches, it waits.
The day unfolds but there is no sun
to brighten the emptiness within.

Minutes creep into hours and with
each passing one, the shadows grow longer.
It tries to grab the remaining warmth only
to find that there was none.

Darkness falls, the chill settles in.
It feels the emptiness echo from the very
core of it's being - with no escape in sight.

Nothing helps to dispel the gloom and
sadness.

- *Mary Alice Hocking*

The Snowflake

I sit here at my table, not even yet awake
Everything is quiet as I stare out the window in a daze
I watch the snowflakes from the Heaven's falling down
They're not falling softly, yet blowing all around
Why is it so hard for them to reach their final goal
To accumulate on the ground as we admire them with awe
The wind comes down and grabs them from their final destiny
In the midst of the snowstorm the single flake is me
I have goals, and dreams, and paths I must take
But trials, like the wind, swoop down and yank me away
One solace I have as I stare out the window now
Is that each snowflake eventually falls to the ground
Resting with the other flakes, its journey now seems done
Until the wind roars again, picks it up and it's gone
That hard, continuous battle is on yet again
But, as in my life, did it ever really end
Yes, the snowflake had just enough time to rest
To gather its countenance for the next wind to test
And, somehow, remains a beauty for all to see
Yes, we're a lot alike, the snowflake and me.

-    *Kim Helton*

Man, Transformed #3

to live and love and lose the game
to wonder freely and forget thy name
to nap in green meadows under clear blue skies
to play with loved ones, telling only tactful lies
to flounder at the hand of regret
to follow one's heart or to simply forget

that to live, and love, and lose it all,
a man, transformed, into a wall —
a wall of granite, so solid and cool,
a wall of sanity, now broken — the fool.

-   *John M. Grohol*

Cast Adrift

Cast adrift
On tides of words
That grow cold in the telling

Frozen bones
Jagged and bent
Hold only my head above the surge

Throw me a line
Help me back inside
Warm me with your melody

Bombarded, beaten, spent
I withdraw from the sea
Defeated

Throw me a line
Help me back inside
Warm me with your melody

-    *Kerry Lafferty*

You Came Blowing My Way

Just like warm weather... you came blowing my way.
At a time when stages stun me, it was one of
those moody-blue days.
The feelings confused, the eyes with a little
less sparkle...

Yes, the time was right for another new step,
whether being up or down... I did not care.
For the sun shone somewhat brighter and the
snow had melted away... back in those spring
ending, summer beginning, adventurous days.

Oh...how I needed a shoulder to lean on.
You came just like warm weather... blowing my way.
You filled up that space in my empty heart,
and your breath on my lips gave light to my eyes
... as we danced in the heat of the moment.

I knew all along, but it still broke my heart,
when winter came... and like the blustery winds...
you blew out of my life one day.
We had our moment, for which I'm glad...because
when its all said and done, only moments really matter....
                                    and spring is just a breath away.
Who knows what might come blowing my way?

- *lady26*

What My Life Is

My Life is like a caterpillar
Going slowly in the mean world
Moving my many legs trying to move quickly from the world

I rest in my cocoon of depression
Curled away from the mean world
In my own world of darkest and quiet

One day I will awake
Awake to the Beauty that I am
A Beautiful Butterfly I am

    -   *Lisa L. Turner*

Take Back Your Sorry Genes

i'm slumped over again,
chin in my hand.
too tired for talking and
not up for crying.
feeling like pummeling
someone with our pain.
someone down the block
who plans rejection again.
the fourth little girl
to fall from his tree.
the fourth to look up to him
as he cuddles jim beam

-    *fayerody*

Just a Hole in the Road

Day after Day you roll over Me
So heavy on me I start to crack
Day after Day getting Bigger
Water starts to fill my cracks

Day after Day I start to break away
Pieces of me start to break apart
Day after Day you start to see a hole
Becoming Deeper and Deeper

Day after Day you roll over Me
I fill with water now when it rains
Day after Day you start to avoid Me
Workmen patch me over

Day after Day you roll over Me
But I am not strong anymore
Day after Day I fall apart more
The workman come again and take me away
Take me away to make a new road
Now I'm gone
Just a memory in drivers minds.

-      *Lisa L. Turner*

Beautiful Day

Beautiful blue, not a cloud in the sky
Somehow feel like I can fly
White swans skimming, their grace I feel
Serene image... so surreal
Brilliant sunset lights the sky on fire
No one could see this and not be inspired
Wind from the woods carries a pleasant scent
Peaceful and calm... my Creator's intent
Look deep inside searching for the same
Deep in my soul I utter His name
Dear God up in Heaven please light the way
For me to escape from all these dark days
My God up in Heaven, way up above
Shine down on me your radiant love
Fill me with peace and send me a sign
Help me to make all these dreams become mine

-    *Ryan McMahon*

The Sun is Setting

The sun is setting
the moon is getting high
People with lives
are passing me by

I raise a silent, lonely, thumb

I crave for someone to see me
To see that I'm real
To give me a chance
To show that I can feel

My whole body rocks in the wind
Yet impassive I stand
Someone will stop
And give me a hand

The sun starts to rise
I've been stood here all night
No one came near me
That boy don't look right

I'm still waiting for help
As the world passes me by
I'll continue to stand here
Watching life pass me by

-   *Simon Raistrick*

21 Years This Day

a man was born a child
twenty-one years ago today
to a family in a suburb
ordinary in ev'ry way.

the best of friends
we grew up to be
sharing so much happiness
in our memory.

in bad times and good
finding ways to keep in touch
drifted apart in college years
didn't talk nearly as much.

twenty-one years, this day
my best friend was given birth
but just twenty-one hours ago
he was buried in this sad earth.

only twenty-one years old —
he took his own life, locked up in his car
listening to a song on the radio, smoking his favorite cigars.

his decision I cannot respect
his actions, not understood
friends and family gathered 'round
trying the best that they could.

twenty-one years ago
a suicide's life was born
yet before i knew he was lost
we all discovered that he was torn.

twenty-one years, this day
my best friend opened the door
and twenty-one hours ago
he died so that he could soar.

-    *John M. Grohol*

Wronged

I need to get out of my head
I need to be somebody else
I want to sleep at night
Without you there

Waking me up
Believing you are waiting
To do it again

As I beg you to stop
And momma pretends not to hear
Wondering why you don't touch her
Like you touch your "special boy"

Is that why she hit me so hard
Is that why she hit me so much

Jealous you "loved" me more

Shamed she didn't help
And turned the other way

Did she beat her guilt out of me
Time and time again

Remembering what she didn't want to see

Hoping I was to young to recall her
Walking away- leaving me
To fend for myself

I need to get out of my head
I need to be somebody else

I want to be free from your smell
There in my waking moments
I smell you at any given time
Out of nowhere you are suddenly there
Consuming me again like when I was four

I relive it there as I get change for
                              my groceries
I am a grown man as seen by others
And yet I am four years old again

Being "loved" by his father
Its happening as it happened there
The clerk looks at me strangely
Wondering why I am sweating
As I rush to my car chased by you

You follow me still
I can not run, I can not hide

You are there
You are always there
You are my disease
You are "loving" me all the time

In my head, in my head
But I feel it to, I feel it to
No one can understand this hell
They blame me for this
They think it's easy to forget

They don't know I am imprisoned
They don't know I try
I try so hard

I don't like this
I hate you
I can't escape you

Don't they think I would
If I could
Oh, if only I could

I would love to be like others
Without you there
Every minute
Reminding me I am your toy
Do they think I enjoy the pain in my ___
Do they think I like to feel you in my ___
Decades after last you "loved" it
Still I feel it
Don't they know I don't want

Don't they know it shouldn't be there
Do they think I like to smell you
Smell your sweat like when you held me down
Suffocated in my pillow
You wouldn't let me scream
You wouldn't let me breathe

Do they think I try to keep
Memories of you in my throat
As I gag and puke
Remembering your slime
Sliding down my
Virgin throat

Do they think I like to remember
Do they think that I really want this hell
Why do they believe I can stop it
When I couldn't stop it then
How easy to say it's easy

When their idea of love is a hug
And my idea of love
is daddy making "love"

Find me the cure
Cuz I don't want to be me
I don't want to be me

I need to be somebody else
I need to get out of my head

- *Vulgerlove*

No Separation

We started off as friends,
Our chats silly and amusing.
Then something happened,
At first it was a little confusing.
Our chats were no longer just friends,
They become so much more.
You quickly became a person,
That I cherish and adore.
You give me many laughs,
Bring many smiles upon my face.
You know all of my faults,
Yet it's me you still embrace.
It seems too good to be true,
Soon we shall find out.
We'll find out each others fault,
Find out what this love is all about.
Until that time comes,
A screen will separate us physically.
But our minds and souls,
Can still run together freely.

- *Stacy Roach*

Sitting in a Full-Throttle Plastic Pew

Kerouac's on the roof sucking sacramental
                              draughts
Of sweet fever-dream nicotine
Deep into tar-stained right-brained
Shivering silky synaptic webs
As curling Holy Ghost wisps
Of smoky soul
Flow from his lips
Like evanescent exhaust haunting
Dead and dying asphalt anaconda curves
Unable to shed their sun-split skin
Along the shredded blistered surface
Of Route 66's gray and crackled
Wind-swept snaking scales of tattered tar.

And he's leaning on a bruised brick wall
With the skeletal metallic blackened bones
Of fire escapes frozen in mid-slither
Up the dinosaur-hide sides of prehistoric
                              tenements
Visible over his shoulder,
A ratty copy of a locomotive brakeman's
                              manual
Protruding like a Bible from the jacket pocket
Of a pit-stop preacher whose pedal-to-the-
                              metal gospel
Is the revelation and elation of sheer
Unmotivated motion.

His supercharged sleek slicked-back hair
Suggests speed even as he slouches
                              motionless,
A gearshift-muscled and gasoline-blooded
Engine of savage street Beat energies,

Captured in restless tense pensive repose
By Allen Ginsberg's Kodak Brownie's shutter
On an overcast long-past afternoon in '53
Mere months before "On the Road"
Rolled off the presses
Like the roaring soaring purr
Of a V-8 engine tuned
To goddamned near perfection,
And transformed him from urban urchin
To highway troubadour,
The piston-driven paramour
Of pavement salvation
Leading to God knows where,
And the hectic electric ecstasy
Of the getting from here to there
Without ever having to arrive anywhere.

Sitting in a full-throttle plastic pew
Wrapped in a romantic's steel cathedral,
Playing whining high-pitched hymns
On an organ of white-walled wheels
That growl bluesy high-octane spirituals,
Chrome fiery choirs singing
To unquiet minds like my own,
As I fix my inner gaze
On the far side of secret horizons
That promise an elastic trip-the-light-fantastic
Rocket-fueled fandango with four-on-the-floor
And one blissful moment of nitro-burning
                              rapture
'Cause, when you get down to it,
Man, that's all I'm asking for.

-   *The Cheshire Cat*

Getting On

Barely grey
So young, they say
He drags himself to work.

Quenched and fed
He feels so dead
Warm greetings yield a smirk.

He loves his wife
But not his life
He barely sleeps, I'm told.

Wrinkle free
No one could see
He feels so fucking old.

- *Christopher Hall*

Do You Wanna Play Ball with Me Daddy?

Do you wanna play ball with me, daddy?
Just toss it for a while?
Do you wanna play a friendly game, daddy?
Or am I to catch it with my bare hands?
Will the ball soar beautifully through the air, daddy?
Or will you throw it with anger and force?
Can I use a glove for protection, daddy?
Or do you want me to anticipate the pain?
Will you hit me with the ball, daddy?
If I fail to reach out my blood-blistered hand?
I play ball as good as I ever will, daddy
So why do you continue to push so much?
Do you really want me to be good, daddy?
Because, now it's your turn to catch
Do you wanna play ball with me, daddy?
Oh, by the way, this time I hid YOUR glove.

-    *Kim Helton*

Back In the Day

back in the day
-along the road
i think we all travel
just
crossing different paths
making us who we are a result
of encountering the unexplained

back in the day
-along that road
I thought I knew it all
having it all figured out
little did I know
that little did I know at all

back in the day
-along that road
Dead ends became second nature
taking me further from
any starting point
to get on track

back in the day
-I lived a different life
learning as I was taught
in each encounter
with each emotion
felt and unfelt

back in the day
-along that road
found redemption
and I found salvation
no longer afraid to coexist
and no longer resentful

back in the day
-I healed and I grew stronger
as the tides got stronger
I grew more determined

back in the day
-what seemed like a problem
now serves only as a challenge
believing in myself
and believing in the lessons I
learned
back in the day

-     *Vulgerlove*

The Hero

Once I abandoned
all intent to steal it, the
golden fleece stole me.

- *Sqrlb8*

Sight

Something has happened to my sense
Of sight. I am seeing old people
Suddenly young. A girl pushing
Her Zimmer frame turns a grey face
To me shyly and I find myself
Flirting. Another rests in her chair
In the sun like a cat, waiting
To be stroked. I can't help
Smiling.

Something has happened to my sense
Of sight, and this is something
That I like.

- *Myzen*

My River #2

I see the death all around
I can see the things I used to love dying all around
I can feel the earth, crumble as I walk down this river
Where did all the water go?
Where did all the life go?

For this reason I will no longer love
For this reason I will no longer live
For this reason I will no longer breath,
For this reason I will take no more on, nor will I even try
I wont go to walk alone again
I wont go out alone
I wont, give of myself
I wont let others in
I wont share my pain
I will keep it locked on the inside
I wont share it for all it does is hurt others
I wont share, my feelings, for I hurt to many already

I am sorry, for my river
for it once was beautiful, vibrant. and full of love

I can feel the cuts on my feet, for they are bare
I can see the blood running off them
I can feel the cuts on my feet, and feel the pain ebbing through them
Oh how i want to cut, again
Oh how I want to finish off this ungodly existence.
I want my river to be full again
I want the blood to go away
I want my fish to live in water, not dust
I want the trees to be green again
I want the flowers to bloom again. (Pollen and all)
I want my birds to sing happy sounds again
not just of death
I want the sun to shine down instead of the dull gray sky...

-   *Patricia Bell*

On the Shore

On a cold and
cloudy mornin',
a broken man stood on the shore.

Head hangin' down,
he cried out,
"Lord, I just can't take it anymore.

"Sure, I hear what
good people say,
but I just can't see it that'a way.

"Aw, I been cryin'
all these years and
now I just can't shed another tear."

Ain't the truth like
wind in your hair,
something that is and is not there?

"My whole life time,
hurryin' nowhere,
and all the time I was already there."

On a cold and
cloudy mornin',
the waves rolled on the shore.

- *Sqrlb8*

You Cannot Turn Back

"The innocence and naiveté of ignorance is gone, and once you've crossed that threshold, you can never turn back"

What an utterly complicated and sad realization that is for me
For there is a definite bliss in ignorance.
Today, I walked outside and looked up to the Heavens, and while searching the vastness there, I saw the sun brightly shining.
However, while studying the orb with a degree of awe, I became uncomfortably aware of the many clouds that surrounded it.
I knew, at that moment, that the clouds would block the warmth and light from the sun, dampening my spirits.
How I longed for the time that I would go outside and look up to the same sky and see only the sun on a partly cloudy day.
That feeling only lasted for a moment, though.
Because I know that when, even in ignorance, I saw only the sun, I felt the effects of the clouds.
Not seeing them, yet feeling so cold, damp and enveloped in complete darkness, without any understanding as to why.
Was I an awful person not to appreciate the beauty offered me?
Was I unappreciative of the comforts bestowed to me?
Why do I still try to decide which is better for me...ignorance or knowledge, knowing that I no longer have that choice?

Because...
"The innocence and naiveté of ignorance is gone, and once you've crossed that threshold, you can never turn back"

- *Kim Helton*

My Desire

I'm the desire who Loves you
Who shows you to Love the pieces great and small
Finds the sunsets at the end of the day to smile about
I make you understand the meaning of it all
Hold you tight to protect you from it all
I Love you even though you hate me so
I stand up for you and face you head on
I'm the desire within

- *Lisa L. Turner*

little girl

A little girl so sad
her smile can't hide-
the tears

-her hopelessness
for a life like other little girls

with one mom
and
one dad

As she grows through the years
her voice is not loud enough
to be heard

she needs her daddy
as much as her mommy

Rejected she feels
among other little girls

years could pass slow
depression could consume her
crashing her world

abandoned she feels

beginning, too young, to obtain
her father's love
through an older man

-Who will destroy
the little girl's innocence
the little girl's world

As

someone taught her
she can not trust
she can not be loved
like others

Someone
proved her unworthy
to be named a daughter
to have a father

Her needs don't matter

And for what purpose
Must the little girl suffer

at night she cries
a worn photograph
hidden beneath her pillow
always asking her daddy why

Constant self doubts

was she ugly
was she dumb
did she do something bad
what if she would of been a
boy

Who can ever love the little girl
if not her own father

she's empty inside
days of play are hard
to pretend to belong

believing her friends
will desert her too
in time

she doesn't know the answers
she only feels the pain

the unknown shame
it must be her fault
for little girl doesn't know
why daddy can't come and
play

But

what if she knew
-that daddy wants to see her
-that daddy tries
and that daddy cries at night
missing his baby girl

no one tells the little girl why

why must the little girl suffer
from mommy's discord

why, mommy, why, the little girl
asks

mommy knows what's best (for
mommy)
mommy is the boss
mommy blames it on daddy

as she ignores the phone
and the little girl wonders
why he doesn't call

mommy says little girl is sick
as outside she plays
Denying her her father's love

And for what purpose
must the little girl suffer
do you not like the little girl?

All grown up
wise beyond her years
taught the hard way
daddy's love doesn't
come easy

Time passes
Little girl finds
the truth

mommy no longer golden

Little girl angry
Little girl ruined

Mommy why
Mommy why

"I HATE YOU! I HATE YOU!"

Mommy loses her little girl
Mommy regrets the lies
Mommy can't go back

Her little girl-she ruined
Her little girl-she lost

little girl wouldn't come back
and mommy knows it all her
fault
and it's too late

-    *Vulgerlove*

Cheshire Cats Like Me Flash Smiles

Playing croquet in Central Park
With live pink flamingo mallets
Is thirsty work, I need refreshments
As does my tattooed pierced friend Alice
And the Walrus and the Carpenter
Recall the fall of NASDAQ's palace
While the Hatter in Trump Tower
Screams, "You're fired!" with snide malice.

In an Avenue A back alley
The Jabberwocky's high on crack
And he's in the crosshairs of Crips hired
By a Bandersnatch blissed on smack
But the White Rabbit was so twitchy
I had to give him a Xanax snack
Before I stole and pawned his pocket watch
To a dormouse who drives a hack.

Deep in the shadows of the 6 line
Where the magic mushrooms grow,
A pimpin' caterpillar's sitting pretty
Amid the yuppies on the go
Watching with psychedelic smugness
As they trundle to and fro,
Tweedledees and Tweedledums
Swept in the subway current's flow.

"Off with their heads!" squawks the Queen,
Her bag-lady court in a grocery cart,
But all the chessman just say, "Up yours,"
And keep on truckin' for their part.
Mayor Humpty-Dumpty's strutting,
A shell trying to look smart
But Cheshire Cats like me flash smiles
And stay hazy and apart.

- *The Cheshire Cat*

Momma-Child

I remember the smell of your chicken frying on Sunday
And how beautiful you looked when we went to church.
I can see the tiredness in your eyes as you struggled through
Night school and still had to do all the work at home.
I remember how desperately you tried to protect
When Dad got vicious and brutal.
I know now how hard it must have been to stay with him
Just so we could have a home.

You made so many sacrifices and you struggled so hard
But you were always strong.
Dad once proudly said you'd charge Hell with a broom
If you thought you were right.
That's the Momma I remember.

Illness and grief have changed you before my eyes.
No longer certain, no longer sure of anything.
Small decisions loom as large problems.
Large problems mushroom into impossible situations.
Your money, the house, almost everything is gone.
Prey to well meant wishes.
Made before I realized you couldn't
Decide those things for yourself anymore.

Now I help make the decisions,
Left to clean up the messes.
You need me, you resent me so much.
What am I going to do?
All at once I am the parent
And you are the child.
I need you, Momma.
Where are you?

    -   *Bonnie O'Hara*

The Bird Preferred Gravity

In its' majesty it bore also
a saturnine valence
of mortality stinging
like nettles
its' mental unbalance

Perceiving itself
downy in daylight it saw
no earthly shadow but was
the thrall of its' own wing
span kept it forever callow

As sole trustee of its' object
it became driven to share
the story of glory it would cause
once it took to the air

So night after night it would
preface its' flight overwriting
the margins
on sheets of foolscap
to be the bound harbinger

Only for no quill it plucked
each new feather was sprouting
plus pooled its' bloodshed for red
ink to draw the account in

Till dawn it would chew its'
raw feather ends
making the shape with its' beak
of the calligraphers' pen

Mourning ink turns to syrup
as scabs seal the soars
it nurses itself to nest on
hardtack and cider it snores
to more heights it won't reach
never knowing its' own shadow
it casts in its' sleep

     -     *kathyanita*

Dig It

Dig it as the multi-platinum,
Shock-and-awe and flatten 'em,
Saks Fifth Avenue Manhattan 'em,
Prized Super-Size and fatten' em,
Orwell-prophesized go rat on 'em,
Dapper fat cat go top hat on 'em,
Grab police batons and bat on 'em,
Ignored the poor and spat on 'em,
Take away the welcome mat on 'em,
Make war not love and Patton 'em,
Elasticize lies to silk and satin 'em,
Red and blue states trade tit-for-tat on 'em,
Boil the oil and dump the vat on 'em
Nation stamps on brain cells that go splat on 'em.

-    *The Cheshire Cat*

Baby

I heard a little girl crying while lying alone in my room
From where her cries came I hadn't a clue
As I struggled to listen, I could hear her repeat
Words of unmeasured fear, mixed with utter defeat
She asked so many questions, but no one ever tried
To calm her fears or wipe dry her pretty eyes
She was forced to endure things no child should face
And was left alone to deal with them in a cold, empty place
She could not react when out in the big, cruel world
Only more harm would come then, of that she was sure
I wanted so to reach out and take her in my arms
To offer some comfort and shelter from any possible harm
I groped for her in the still, black night
But I couldn't reach her, so I turned on the light
I looked all around the room, but she couldn't be seen
And I wondered aloud if it was all just a dream
Today I know this - she's real and somewhere near
Because that little girl's cry still rings loud in my ear

-     Kim Helton

Hungry Ghosts

Hungry ghosts will always have their hooks
To slip inside your skin and quickly catch
You whole, and it is this that they want
For the feeding which they must be doing.

These ghosts will spend much time
Pretending to be not hungry, but this
Is only waiting to them, for they are hungry,
Hungry ghosts, and this is all they know.

The hooks, at first unsighted, slip in
Easily, and painless too with the
Anaesthetic of the flattering and the
Host comforted and already lost.

And suddenly we are strapped down tight
Once they know we don't have the fight
In us and they can show their knives
To do the feeding which they must be doing.

The hungry ghosts will feed and
Feed on other's flesh and find no
Comfort there for all they have is
Hunger, there is nothing spared or given.

This feeding I have seen and done myself
For I was hungry once in just this way,
Flashing my shiny hooks at all until one fell
And I could fall upon them.

I was a hungry ghost and I did
Learn this one lesson, simply
That hunger sated will regrow,
There is no end to be found in hunger, only
The feeding which we must be doing.

    -    *Myzen*

Lovers Pain

You're constantly on my mind,
Day in and day out.
I want you here with me,
I want you to feel what this love is about!
Seems like yesterday,
We were happily together.
God I miss your sexy voice,
Your sweet little whisper.
I miss the way you held me,
I miss the way you said, "I Love You".
I miss everything about us,
Our love was so real and true.
I was looking through old pictures,
Came across your beautiful face.
My heart dropped as I realized,
No one will ever take your place.
Every person I'm with,
They are always compared to you.
Truth is they don't measure up,
No matter what they ever do.
I hope fate brings us together again,
I want no other than you.
When you're ready I'm here waiting,
Ready to say, "I Do".

- *Stacy Roach*

Spider

I am ignorant of you
Until you hurry into my path
What business has brought you into my house
So urgent that you must scurry?

I step upon you, obliterating your life
And scrape your carcass off my soul
And it is as if you never were
Your business is undone

And I know that a beast will come in time
A great one, but without malice
And will smash me into nothing
And will see the insignificance of my end.

-    *Julie Gordon*

crumbs

that's all i'm worth; all that I expect, all that I deserve.

i'm not real - not a real client, a real friend, a real person.

just a shadow, really. if you happen to see me, toss me a bone or some leftovers. that's all i ask. i'm already guilty enough for asking that much.

i should be strong enough to take care of myself.

i should be invisible enough that you don't know i'm there. then you could save the crumbs for the dogs - who are probably more deserving anyway.

i wish that I could fade away; disappear; not exist. then i could stop pestering you with my pleadings for crumbs that I don't deserve, after all.

-   *Rapunzel*

Recurring Nightmare

Walking through the door of broken dreams,
I wander through familiar, lovely rooms.
Various are decorated Gothic style,
many others in Contemporary,
yet the last wing was opulent, eclectic.

Weariness is heavy, overcomes me,
searching for the door from which I entered.
It seems my way was lost long before
leaving foyer and entering the corridor.
Wasn't it carpeted before, or broken planks bare then?

Climbing staircases that go down, I struggle
in search of loved, familiar faces.
This music hall wasn't here before!
John smiling, waving from distant balcony.
Should I jump or keep searching for the door?

In quest of absent terrace entrance,
Bounding down staircases that go up,
In a university strangely familiar
Yet, never having heard its name before,
Karla stomps a scolding foot,
"Aren't you aware we're late, or do you care?"

Anguish and frustration cripple me.
What I want is to leave, exit once and all
This eternal tangle of disconnected rooms.
Where is the hallway that logic demands?
No passage, just room upon room.
Familiar fades, chamber becomes another.
If I could find the passage, I know I'd find the door!

Elusive elevators that only go one floor,
Just deplaned one and now it's gone!
Clowns, mannequins leering at me, lead
Through garish china shops, vogue garment stores.
John's children play, one baby caring for the other,
But where is he? ... and Karla won't forgive me.

Is this still the seventh mezzanine?
Room within a tunnel but waiting for a passageway.
Jeering mannequins befriend me,
"Follow me and I shall lead you to the exit."
It's closing time, but I've yet to find the door!

-    *Tomi Inglis*

The Mirror

Looking into the mirror
What do I see?
Many people
One body.

Don't know where I've been
Don't know where I'm going
Time passes by
All in a blur.

Looking into the mirror
What do I see?
A shimmering shadow
Neither here nor there.

Don't know who I am
Don't know if I'm real
What am I gonna do
When I no longer feel.

Looking into the mirror
What do I see?
A fuzzy image
Of hope that never was.

Don't know why I burn
Don't know how to stop
Pain lasts forever
Rage explodes with fury.

Looking into the mirror
What do I see?
A smiling mask
Hiding the scars.

Don't know where I am
Don't know how I got here
I can be an angel when feeling high
But the devil inside rules this mind.

Looking into the mirror
What do I see?
No reflection
No more hope.

Don't know how to cope
Don't know where to go
Death is my salvation
My only control.

Looking into the mirror
What do I see?
This hell I leave
For eternal peace.

-        *SS8282*

In the Deep Woods

Darkness Falls
So cold you can't move
No way out
The voices stay with you
Somewhere in the deep woods

You start to run
Still alone
You start to fall
If only to find where you are
Somewhere in the deep woods

Someone is there
Little friend who runs away
Just to hold something
Someone safe and warm
Somewhere in the deep woods

Voices run
Hiding from everyone
Never to find you
Loneliness again
Somewhere in the deep woods

You see them
If only they could see you
Voices you leave there
Voices from inside standing there before you
Somewhere in the deep woods the voices live.

- *Lisa L. Turner*

she sits alone

she sits alone
cold and scared
trapped within her mind
she locked the doors long ago
when no one was around.

now the windows are clearer
and reality seems fair
but through a choice made long ago
she'll remain hidden in there.

the lock has long been rusted
the doors have been sealed shut
regardless of the view outside
she remains trapped in there.

banging on the door
pleading to be free
is a pointless waste of energy
she'll die alone in there.

- *John M. Grohol*